Descriptosaurus Punctuation in Action Year 1: The Ninjabread Girl

The Gingerbread Man was rather a handful, but wait until you meet the Ninjabread Girl! With a "Hiiiiii-yaaaaa!" she runs away saying, "Run! Run! So fast like a twirl ... you can't catch me, I'm the Ninjabread Girl!" Can the Ninjutsu Trainer catch her? What about the crocodile? Or the wolf? Can nothing stop her?

On her journey, the Ninjabread Girl writes the story with the assistance of the fox spirit Kitsune and Punctua, the Fairy Godmother of Writing, to punctuate properly and become a bestselling author.

Descriptosaurus Punctuation in Action Year 1: The Ninjabread Girl is part of a short series of age-specific, beautifully illustrated stories that can be read for pleasure and/or used as a contextualised resource, containing a step-by-step guide to teaching punctuation. The characters from each story are used to demonstrate a range of punctuation rules in a fun and engaging way appropriate to the book's age group. Areas covered include:

- ★ formulating punctuation rules.
- ★ the use of misconceptions to highlight common errors.
- ★ teaching tips to provide a punctuation model.

The book explores the impact of punctuation on reading, understanding, meaning and effect, and can be used as a basis for pupils' own punctuation or included in their 'Writer's Toolkit.' These new *Descriptosaurus* stories are an indispensable teaching aid for making punctuation fun for all primary teachers and literacy coordinators.

Adam Bushnell is an award-winning and Amazon number one best-selling author of fictional and academic books. He works in the UK and internationally in both state and private education delivering creative writing workshops to all ages. His books have been selected by the School Library Association for the "Boys into Books" recommended reading list. Previously a teacher, Adam also delivers CPD to teachers and others working in education on how to inspire writing in the classroom.

Descriptosaurus Punctuation in Action Year 1

The Ninjabread Girl

Adam Bushnell

Routledge
Taylor & Francis Group
LONDON AND NEW YORK

First published 2022
by Routledge
2 Park Square, Milton Park, Abingdon, Oxon OX14 4RN

and by Routledge
605 Third Avenue, New York, NY 10158

Routledge is an imprint of the Taylor & Francis Group, an informa business

British Library Cataloguing-in-Publication Data
A catalogue record for this book is available from the British Library

Library of Congress Cataloging-in-Publication Data
Names: Bushnell, Adam, author.
Title: Descriptosaurus punctuation in action year 1: the ninjabread girl/Adam Bushnell.
Description: Abingdon, Oxon; New York, NY: Routledge, [2022] |
Identifiers: LCCN 2021008207 | ISBN 9781032040820 (hardback) |
ISBN 9781032040844 (paperback) | ISBN 9781003190455 (ebook)
Subjects: LCSH: English language–Punctuation–Juvenile literature.
Classification: LCC PE1450 .B86 2022 | DDC 428.2/3–dc23
LC record available at https://lccn.loc.gov/2021008207

ISBN: 9781032040820 (hbk)
ISBN: 9781032040844 (pbk)
ISBN: 9781003190455 (ebk)

DOI: 10.4324/9781003190455

Typeset in Myriad Pro
by Deanta Global Publishing Services, Chennai, India

Contents

Dedication and acknowledgement

For my friends and my family for all of their continued support.

Thanks also to the wonderful creator of the *Descriptosaurus* series, Alison Wilcox. She has been my guide, my teacher and my source of inspiration.

A big thanks to Bruce Roberts and Molly Selby of Routledge for their encouragement and guidance.

Huge thanks to the amazing and talented illustrators Nigel Clifton and Dani Pasteau for their contribution to this book.

Introduction

Research has demonstrated the negative impact SPAG (spelling, punctuation and grammar) has had on creativity. It has also revealed that the knowledge and application required in the context of the test have not resulted in a marked improvement in the quality of pupils' written texts, as it is decontextualised and places emphasis primarily on identification and labelling. It does not, therefore, equip young writers to apply their knowledge of punctuation in their own writing, or, more specifically, assist them in developing a system for editing their own texts. In response, the new Ofsted Framework has focused on being able to demonstrate pupil progress in the writing process, which includes pupils being able to revise and edit their own written work.

Resources are, therefore, required to demonstrate models and support pupils with understanding the editing process, as well as developing their knowledge of writing conventions. In addition to providing models in the context of a short story, there is a need for young writers to be able to investigate, discuss and explore texts to assess the impact of punctuation on the reading and understanding of a text.

Whilst most punctuation resources provide models, it is a useful exercise for pupils to be presented with incorrect punctuation so that they can begin to understand the importance of communicating a clear meaning and can use that knowledge and understanding when editing their own texts. Each of the punctuation sections in these short stories will examine rules, misconceptions and common errors as well as providing punctuation models.

The *Descriptosaurus: Punctuation in Action* series are companion books to *Descriptosaurus Story Writing: Language in Action*, which was designed to combine the need to develop descriptive vocabulary for a wide range of settings and characters with models of story, sentence structure and grammar, as well as exercises to scaffold pupils as they innovate and invent their own models. There are four stories in the series: *The Ninjabread Girl, Captain Moody and His Pirate Crew, Ruby Red* and *Jack and the Crystal Fang*. Each story has been written in a different style and with the curriculum needs of each year group in mind. The individual stories can be used, innovated and deconstructed according to the level, experience and knowledge of each age group, class or individual.

The story of *The Ninjabread Girl* can be used for "reading for pleasure" but also contains a section on punctuation. The aim is to demonstrate punctuation in the context of a story and with characters that will have become familiar from reading the story. The characters are used to demonstrate a range of punctuation rules appropriate to the targeted age group:

1. formulating punctuation rules
2. using misconceptions to highlight common errors
3. using teaching tips to provide a punctuation model

They can be used as a basis for pupils' own punctuation posters and cards, or copied to include in their 'Writer's Toolkit.'

THE NINJABREAD GIRL

Part A: The story of The Ninjabread Girl

The Ninjabread Girl takes the traditional tale of the Gingerbread Man and retells an alternative story. The structure and plot are the same but we meet characters from Japanese folklore such as Kitsune, the fox spirit. We also meet a Ninjutsu trainer, a crocodile, a wolf and a dragon, who chase the Ninjabread Girl. Then she comes to a river but cannot cross it. Suddenly, Kitsune offers to swim her across.

Part B: Learning punctuation with the characters

On her journey, the Ninjabread Girl writes her story with the assistance of Kitsune and Punctua (the Fairy Godmother of Writing) to punctuate properly and become a bestselling author.

Part A

The story of The Ninjabread Girl

1

The Ninjabread Girl

DOI: 10.4324/9781003190455-1

Once upon a time, there was a Ninjutsu trainer who decided to make a Gingerbread Girl. He gave her currants for eyes and cherries for her buttons. Then he gave her a black liquorice suit.

The Ninjutsu trainer put the Gingerbread Girl into the oven to bake.

When the smell of gingerbread filled the kitchen, the Ninjutsu trainer opened the oven door. Out leapt the Gingerbread Girl with a "Hiiiiii-yaaaaa!"

The Gingerbread Girl ran straight past her maker and with a kick and a jump, leapt straight through an open window then out into the garden.

"Run! Run! So fast like a twirl … you can't catch me, I'm the Ninjabread Girl!"

The Ninjutsu trainer chased the Ninjabread Girl across the garden and down into the lane.

Just then she ran into a big, bad crocodile, who said, "Stop! Stop! I want to eat you up!"

"Run! Run! So fast like a twirl … you can't catch me, I'm the Ninjabread Girl!" replied the little ninja.

The crocodile began to chase the Ninjabread Girl along with the Ninjutsu trainer.

The Ninjabread Girl ran on a little further and met a huge, angry wolf who said, “Stop! Stop! I want to eat you up!”

“Run! Run! So fast like a twirl … you can’t catch me, I’m the Ninjabread Girl!” replied the little ninja.

The wolf joined the crocodile and the Ninjutsu trainer chasing the Ninjabread Girl.

But she ran on further still until she met a massive, evil dragon, who said, "Stop! Stop! I want to eat you up!"

"Run! Run! So fast like a twirl … you can't catch me, I'm the Ninjabread Girl!" replied the little ninja.

The dragon, wolf, crocodile and Ninjutsu trainer all chased the Ninjabread Girl down the lane.

She ran on even further until she came to a river.

"Oh no!" cried the Ninjabread Girl, "My training is not yet complete! I cannot yet walk on water, nor can I turn invisible! What will I do? They will catch me!"

Just then, Kitsune, the fox spirit, came along and said, "Jump up on my tail. I shall swim you across the river."

"Do you promise not to eat me?" asked the Ninjabread Girl.

"Of course. I just want to help," smiled Kitsune.

The Ninjabread Girl climbed onto Kitsune's tail. But soon the little ninja began to get wet.

"Climb onto my back," said Kitsune.

So, the Ninjabread Girl did.

As they swam Kitsune said, "You are too heavy. I am tired. Jump onto my nose."

The Ninjabread Girl jumped onto Kitsune's nose!

No sooner had they reached the other side than Kitsune tossed the Ninjabread Girl up in the air. He opened his mouth and "Snap!" That was the end of the Ninjabread Girl!

Part B

Learning punctuation with the characters

2

Meet the characters

Section 1: The Ninjabread Girl

Section 2: Kitsune

Section 3: Punctua (the Fairy Godmother of Writing)

DOI: 10.4324/9781003190455-2

SECTION 1: THE NINJABREAD GIRL

Hi, I'm the Ninjabread Girl, the author of this story. I am delighted with the published story and hope you enjoyed reading it as much as I enjoyed writing it.

I want to say a huge thank you to Punctua, my fairy godmother. Without her assistance, I wouldn't have been able to turn my exciting ideas into a fabulous story that I hope you found easy to read, understand and enjoy.

Whilst Kitsune was annoying, as he picked up all my mistakes, his comments were actually very useful for showing me that it is important to punctuate my writing correctly so that my readers can enjoy the story.

SECTION 2: KITSUNE

Kitsune refused to give an interview, but issued the following statement:

The Ninjabread Girl left the first draft of her story in the mud on the river bank. It was covered in dirt and had loads of mistakes in it. At least she has now learned to look after her work and also now knows how to edit her writing correctly. She has written a good story (with my help, of course).

Kitsune

(the fox spirit and best writer in the world)

SECTION 3: PUNCTUA (THE FAIRY GODMOTHER OF WRITING)

Greetings, readers. I'm Punctua, the Fairy Godmother of Writing. I have worked with all the famous authors over many centuries.

The Ninjabread Girl was a delight to work with. Her ideas were brilliant, and she was keen to learn how to make them clear, exciting and easy to read and understand.

She worked hard every day learning about punctuation until her story was edited correctly and ready for publication and performance. She thoroughly deserves all her success. Well done, Ninjabread Girl, on becoming an international bestselling author.

Punctua

3

Editing a story

Section 1: Writing and editing tips

Section 2: Sentences

Section 3: Comma splicing

DOI: 10.4324/9781003190455-3

SECTION 1: WRITING AND EDITING TIPS

Editing a story

The process:

- ★ Write a first draft.
- ★ Edit: check grammar, spelling and punctuation.

NINJABREAD GIRL'S WRITING TIPS:

I love telling stories – usually about the things that I have done! I love to tell made-up stories too though. The only thing is, I find it hard to write stories. It's not because I don't know what to say, it's just that I always forget to put in punctuation and to check my spellings. If I stop and check that the punctuation and spelling are correct then I lose my story. It pops out of my head!

So, instead, I write the story and then check it afterwards for punctuation and spelling mistakes. When I read it aloud then I can hear where I need to make changes. Sometimes I miss words or put them in the wrong places. But I often miss these mistakes even though I've read my story out loud. So, I ask Punctua to check it too.

To help me with my story editing and my other writing, I've made punctuation rule cards, and have included examples just for you.

Ninjabread Girl xx

PUNCTUA'S POINTS:

When you are editing your writing, **read it aloud** and:

- ★ note when you **pause**.
- ★ put a pencil mark at that point on your text.

Ask:

- ★ Why did I **pause**?
- ★ Was it because:
  - a. the thought, statement, idea or description was **complete**?
  - b. you had to re-read what was written because it **didn't make any sense**?

NINJABREAD GIRL'S FIRST DRAFT:

my name is ninjabread girl and I live in a house with a garden

Editing a story

The first draft:

Read it aloud.

Does it make sense?

Start with checking the sentences for full stops and capital letters.

KITSUNE'S WHINES:

I'm reading this so fast as there are no pauses. Also, isn't Ninjabread Girl a name? Doesn't that need capital letters? I can't spot capital letters anywhere!

I'm finding it too hard to read and understand.

PUNCTUA'S POINTS:

Punctuation is like a series of traffic signals. Without it, words get jammed together, and your writing won't make any sense. It will take your reader a long time to get to the end and they could get terribly lost.

A **full stop** is the most important **punctuation mark**. It helps you to **signal to your reader** that the **sentence has ended,** and the statement (thought, description, idea) is **complete**.

When reading your first draft, ask yourself these questions:

1. Is this a sentence?
2. Does it make **sense**?
3. Is it **complete** or do extra words need to be added?
4. Does it start with a **capital letter** and end with a **full stop**?

In Ninjabread Girl's first draft, there were no full stops or capital letters, and no complete sentences.

my name is ninjabread girl and I live in a house with a garden

1. We need a **capital letter** at the start – **M**y – and a **full stop** at the end.
2. Where is the first complete statement? My name is Ninjabread Girl.
3. Where is the second complete statement? I live in a house.
4. Where is the third complete statement? It is a house with a garden.

Note: Ninjabread Girl has joined the first two points with **and** to **combine them into one sentence**.

So, the first complete sentence should have been:

My name is Ninjabread Girl and I live in a house with a garden.

There is a ***capital letter*** *at the start and a* ***full stop*** *at the end. The two sentences are* ***joined*** *together using* ***and***.

SECTION 2: SENTENCES

Sentences

There are four types of sentences:

- statement (.)
- question (?)
- command/instruction (.)
- exclamation (!)

NINJABREAD GIRL'S RULES:

My house is near a river. **(statement)**

You can't catch me! **(exclamation)**

Can I trust Kitsune? **(question)**

Stop running. **(command)**

KITSUNE'S WHINES:

I'll bet Ninjabread Girl only used full stops in her writing. I'll bet she can't use question marks or exclamation marks where they are needed.

PUNCTUA'S POINTS:

Remember: punctuation marks are a series of traffic signals.

Punctuation marks make it **easier to read** and **understand what has been written** and **how** it is meant to be **read** or **spoken**.

(There are more tips about question marks and exclamation marks later.)

It is true to say that **every sentence ends with a full stop**.

Look closely at the **bottom** of a **question mark** and an **exclamation mark**. What do you notice?

Both have a full stop at the bottom!

Recap:

A **sentence** is a **unit of words** that is **complete** and **makes sense**.

It can be a **statement**, **question**, **exclamation** or **instruction**.

A **sentence** always **starts** with a **capital letter** and **ends** with a **full stop**.

SECTION 3: COMMA SPLICING

Comma splicing

- ★ Commas cannot be used to join two complete sentences.
- ★ Use a conjunction to join two sentences instead.

NINJABREAD GIRL'S RULES:

Sometimes two **sentences** link ideas, thoughts or descriptions and you want to join the sentences together.

A comma *cannot* be used to join two sentences. This is called **comma splicing**.

You need to use a **conjunction** to link the two sentences.

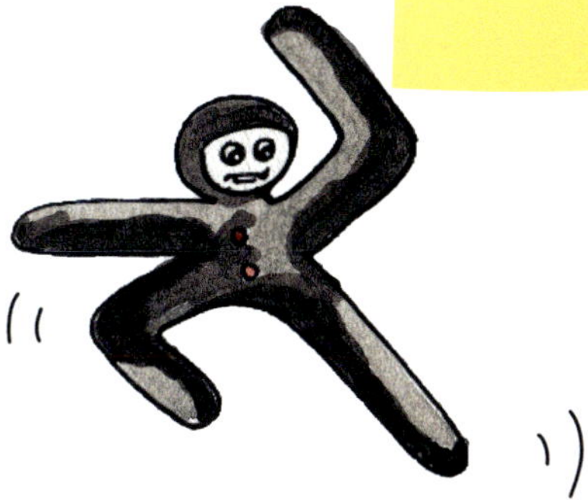

KITSUNE'S WHINES:

Sentence splicing makes sentences sound so strange. They just don't read right.

Ninjabread Girl spliced a sentence when she wrote:

I ran down the lane, I reached a river.

They wanted to eat me, I ran away.

PUNCTUA'S POINTS:

For your writing to flow and not sound jerky, it is important to **vary the length of your sentences**.

But **two complete sentences cannot be joined by a comma**.

You need to use a **conjunction**, for example: **and**, **but**, **so**.

When editing your writing, *check*:

- ★ how many complete statements are included in one sentence?
- ★ have you joined them using a comma or a conjunction?

Examples:

We can link two sentences to:

1. **add another statement** using **and**.

   I ran down the lane **and** I reached a river.

2. **explain the first statement** using **so**.

   They wanted to eat me **so** I ran away.

4

Capital letters

Section 1: Beginning of a sentence and names of people

Section 2: Names of places

Section 3: Days of the week and months of the year

Section 4: Editing checklist

DOI: 10.4324/9781003190455-4

SECTION 1: BEGINNING OF A SENTENCE AND NAMES OF PEOPLE

Capital letters

- ★ start every sentence.
- ★ are used for names of people.

NINJABREAD GIRL'S RULES:

Capital letters are used:

- ★ to start a sentence.
- ★ for the names of people.
- ★ for 'I.'

Examples:

My name is **N**injabread **G**irl. **I** ran away from the **N**injutsu **T**rainer.

KITSUNE'S WHINES:

In the first draft of the story, there were no capital letters for the names of people. Ninjabread Girl wrote **ninjabread girl** and **kitsune**.

PUNCTUA'S POINTS:

Capital letters are **signposts** that help us to understand a text and spot the **characters** and **places** easily.

Ninjabread Girl remembered to **start her sentences** with a capital letter, and she remembered a capital letter for '**I**.'

However, she forgot about the **names of people**.

Ninjabread Girl and **Ninjutsu Trainer** both start with a capital letter, as does **Kitsune**.

SECTION 2: NAMES OF PLACES

Capital letters

- ★ start every sentence.
- ★ are used for names of people and 'I.'
- ★ are used for names of places.

NINJABREAD GIRL'S RULES:

Capital letters are used for:

★ names of **places.**

Examples:

I was born inside a cottage called **N**injutsu **L**odge near **R**aging **R**iver.

KITSUNE'S WHINES:

Ninjabread Girl's first draft had no capital letters for places. She wrote:

I was born in a cottage called ninjutsu lodge near a river called raging river.

How could I know that these were places without capital letters?

PUNCTUA'S POINTS:

Capital letters can help us to spot the **names of places** easily.

Ninjabread Girl forgot that the names of her **cottage** and the **river** nearby both start with capital letters. She needed to add capital letters because they are both names of **places**.

She should have written:

I was born in an oven inside a cottage called **N**injutsu **L**odge. This is near a wide river called **R**aging **R**iver.

SECTION 3: DAYS OF THE WEEK AND MONTHS OF THE YEAR

Capital letters

1. start every sentence.
2. are used for:
   - ★ names of people and 'I.'
   - ★ names of places.
   - ★ days of the week.
   - ★ months of the year.

NINJABREAD GIRL'S RULES:

Capital letters are important. They **start a sentence** and should be used for:

a. names of **people**, as well as '**I**.'
b. names of **places**.
c. **days** of the week.
d. **months** of the year.

KITSUNE'S WHINES:

Capitals are important. So, why do you keep forgetting them? You need them for:

- ★ days of the week.
- ★ months of the year.

PUNCTUA'S POINTS:

I gave this model for Ninjabread Girl to keep in her **Writer's Toolkit**. Whenever she can't remember when to use capital letters, she can use this **model** to help her. It's always useful to have a model to look at when you are editing.

My name is **Ninjabread Girl**. **I** ran away from the **Ninjutsu Trainer** on the last **Saturday** in **August**. This **Saturday** in **August** was the same day that I was born in **Ninjutsu Lodge**.

This is near a wide river called **Raging River**.

SECTION 4: EDITING CHECKLIST

Capital letters

1. start every sentence.
2. are used for:
   - ★ names of people, including 'I.'
   - ★ names of places
   - ★ days of the week.
   - ★ months of the year.

EDITING CHECKLIST:

I found it hard to remember where to put capital letters, so Punctua and I came up with this checklist to use when I am editing.

I take each item one at a time:

1. beginning of every sentence ☐
2. names of people ☐
3. 'I' ☐
4. names of places ☐
5. days of the week ☐
6. months of the year ☐

5

Question marks

DOI: 10.4324/9781003190455-5

Question marks

- ★ go at the end of direct questions.

NINJABREAD GIRL'S RULES:

Question marks go **at the end** of **direct questions**, which usually begin with words like:

Who? What? When?

Why? Where? How?

Is? Are? Can? Will?

KITSUNE'S WHINES:

What do you call someone who believes everything you say?

Who is naughty and runs away from everyone?

Who is always shouting and asking lots of questions, but forgets to put a question mark at the end of the question? Why does she not listen to the Ninjutsu Trainer?

PUNCTUA'S POINTS:

Young writers:

- ★ get **direct** and **indirect questions** confused.
- ★ forget the **question mark** at the **end of the sentence**.

Direct question:

- ★ where the speaker's **exact words are repeated**

For example: **Where** are you going**? Who** did you meet**? When** did you get home**?**

Indirect question:

- ★ where the exact words are **not repeated**

For example:

Kitsune **asked me** where I was going. The Ninjutsu Trainer **asked me** who I had met.

6

Exclamation marks

DOI: 10.4324/9781003190455-6

Exclamation marks

Exclamation marks are used to show:

- ★ surprise.
- ★ an outburst.
- ★ humour.

NINJABREAD GIRL'S RULES:

Exclamation marks signal:

- ★ **surprise**: Oh no! A river!
- ★ **an outburst**: You can't catch me!
- ★ **humour**: What do you call a fox with carrots in his ears? Anything you want as he can't hear you!

KITSUNE'S WHINES:

Ninjabread Girl is always shouting. She emphasises *everything*. She uses exclamation marks in her writing all of the time too. It's like being shouted at!

In her first draft, she put exclamation marks at the end of every sentence, which was really *annoying*!

Did you know exclamation marks were once called *shrieks* – a great name for the noises Ninjabread Girl makes when she is surprised or scared?

PUNCTUA'S POINTS:

Exclamation marks are a **signal** to the reader that the **character** has a **strong emotional reaction** to something.

It could be:

- ★ a **surprise**.
- ★ an **outburst**.
- ★ a **joke**.

Example:

Oh no**!** A river**!**

They are extremely useful for **emphasis** but should **not** be used **too often**.

7

Inverted commas (speech marks)

Section 1: When and how to use inverted commas

Section 2: How to punctuate inside the inverted commas

DOI: 10.4324/9781003190455-7

SECTION 1: WHEN AND HOW TO USE INVERTED COMMAS

Inverted commas (speech marks)

Inverted commas (speech marks) are used to:

- ★ identify dialogue (direct speech).
- ★ enclose the exact words spoken.

Use commas to separate speech from the rest of the sentence.

NINJABREAD GIRL'S RULES:

- ★ Use **inverted commas** or **speech marks** to **quote the exact words** someone has **said**.
- ★ Usually use **"double quotation marks"** (*66* and *99*).

Example:

"My name is Ninjabread Girl."

- ★ **the exact words spoken by me**
- ★ enclosed within **speech marks** at the **beginning** and the **end**

KITSUNE'S WHINES:

In the first draft, Ninjabread Girl wrote:

The Ninjutsu Trainer shouted come back here from the kitchen.

I had difficulty working out what exactly the Ninjutsu Trainer had said.

PUNCTUA'S POINTS:

1. The Ninjutsu Trainer shouted come back here from the kitchen.

To ensure that the reader doesn't get confused about **who is talking** and **what they say**, we need to use **inverted commas** to **separate the speaker** and **their words**.

"Come back here!" (This is what the Ninjutsu Trainer said.)

To **separate the speech from the rest of the sentence** and make it clear **what is being said by whom** we need a **comma**.

The Ninjutsu Trainer shouted from the kitchen, "Come back here!"

We could have put the **speech first**, but we still need an **exclamation mark** to **separate the speech** and the **speaker**.

"Come back here!" Mother shouted from the door.

(Note: the comma or exclamation mark comes inside the speech marks.)

SECTION 2: HOW TO PUNCTUATE INSIDE THE INVERTED COMMAS

Inverted commas (speech marks)

The words a person says always begin with a capital letter.

- ★ Question marks and exclamation marks go inside the speech marks.
- ★ If the quotation ends a sentence, put a full stop before the closing speech marks.
- ★ Start a new line for each new speaker.

NINJABREAD GIRL'S RULES:

1. The words a person says always **begin** with a **capital letter**.

For example:

"**C**limb onto my back," Kitsune said. (Kitsune said, "**C**limb onto my back.")

2. The **question mark** or **exclamation mark** goes **inside the speech marks**.

For example:

"Oh no**!"** I cried. "How will I cross the river**?"**

3. If the **speech ends a sentence**, a **full stop** goes **before the closing speech marks**.

For example:

Kitsune said, **"I** will help you**."**

4. Start a **new line** every time there is a **change** in the **person speaking**.

KITSUNE'S WHINES:

In the first draft, the Ninjabread Girl wrote:

"Oh no. How will I cross the river," I asked. "I will help you" Kitsune said.

PUNCTUA'S POINTS:

It can be very confusing for the reader if dialogue is not punctuated correctly.

Ninjabread Girl needed to break up what she said from what Kitsune said. She should have written:

> "Oh no. How will I cross the river?" I asked.
>
> "I will help you," Kitsune said.

Top tip:

> **Start** the speech using a **capital letter inside the opening speech marks**.
>
> **End** the speech with a **comma**, **full stop**, **question mark** or **exclamation mark inside the closing speech marks**.

8

Apostrophes

DOI: 10.4324/9781003190455-8

SECTION 1: APOSTROPHES FOR POSSESSION

Apostrophes ’

Apostrophes are used to:

- show possession (that something belongs to someone).

NINJABREAD GIRL’S RULES:

An apostrophe (’) + s **shows possession**.

It shows that **something** is **owned** by **someone** or is **connected** to **something**.

For example:

The oven belonging to the Ninjutsu Trainer.

The Ninjutsu Trainer**’s** oven.

The liquorice suit belonging to Ninjabread Girl.

Ninjabread Girl**’s** suit.

KITSUNE’S WHINES:

In the first draft, Ninjabread Girl wrote:

Kitsunes’ teeth.

Seems that she knew an apostrophe had to go somewhere *but* she didn’t know *where*.

She also wrote:

lots of crocodiles’.

PUNCTUA'S POINTS:

1. Kitsune's teeth

   There is only a **single** fox spirit called Kitsune. The teeth **belong** to **one fox spirit called Kitsune**.

   Who **owns** the **teeth**? **Kitsune**.

   Add **'s** to Kitsune = **Kitsune's**, *not* **Kitsunes'**.

2. lots of crocodiles'

   Does anything **belong** to the crocodiles? **No**. No need for an apostrophe.

   lots of **crocodiles** (crocodiles is plural)

NINJABREAD GIRL'S RULES:

If something is owned by more than one person and the plural noun ends in 's':

For example:

The sweets belonging to the **friends**.

friend**s** ends in '**s**'.

Add an **apostrophe** after the 's.'

The **friends'** sweets.

Apostrophes

- Apostrophes are used to show possession.
- For plural nouns ending in 's,' just add an apostrophe after the 's.'

KITSUNE'S WHINES:

In the first draft, Ninjabread Girl wrote:

The flowers's petals were pretty.

The fairies's magic was powerful.

PUNCTUA'S POINTS:

The flowers's petals.

There is **more than one** flower.

The plural of flower is **flowers**. It ends in '**s**.'

As it already ends in 's,' just **add an apostrophe** after the 's.'

★ **the flowers' petals**

The fairies's magic.

The magic belongs to more than one fairy.

The plural of fairy is **fairies**.

It already ends in 's' – **add an apostrophe** after the '**s**.'

★ **fairies' magic**

What if the **plural** noun **doesn't end in 's'**? For example, **women**.

★ You need to add an **apostrophe and 's'**: **women's clothing**

NINJABREAD GIRL'S RULES:

If the something is owned by a **singular noun**, for example, **octopus**, which ends in '**s**':

For example:

A tentacles belonging to an octopus

Octopus already ends in '**s**.'

Add an apostrophe after the 's.'

Example:

- ★ **octopus' tentacles**

Apostrophes

- ★ Apostrophes are used to show possession.
- ★ For singular nouns ending in 's,' just add an apostrophe after the 's.'

KITSUNE'S WHINES:

In the first draft, Ninjabread Girl wrote:

walru's flippers.

rhinocero's horn.

PUNCTUA'S POINTS:

Example: walru's flippers

The flippers belong to the **walrus**.

Walrus is **singular** and **ends in 's**.'

Add an **apostrophe after 's**.'

★ **walrus' flippers**

Example: rhinocero's horn

The horn belongs to the rhinoceros.

Rhinoceros is **singular** and **ends in 's.'**

Add an **apostrophe after 's**.'

★ **rhinoceros' horn**

SECTION 2: APOSTROPHES FOR CONTRACTION

Apostrophes: contractions

Apostrophes are used to show when two words have been joined together.

- ★ Some letters are missing.
- ★ Missing letters are replaced by an apostrophe.

NINJABREAD GIRL'S RULES:

Apostrophes are used to show where the missing letters go when **two words** have been **joined** and **shortened**.

For example:

I'm (I **a**m); you're (you **a**re); she's (she **i**s); it's (it **i**s); they're (they **a**re); he'll (he **wi**ll); can't (can**no**t); don't (do n**o**t); there's (there **i**s)

KITSUNE'S WHINES:

Ninjabread Girl kept making mistakes with where to put the apostrophe for both **can't** and **you're**.

She wrote:

You **ca'nt** catch me! You **cant'** catch me! **Your'e** too slow! **Youre'** too slow!

That is not right, is it, Punctua?

PUNCTUA'S POINTS:

We all make mistakes; it's how we learn! Putting the apostrophe in the right place in words like **can't** and **you're** can be confusing. The more we practise the better we get.

Ninjabread Girl corrected her work and changed it to:

You **can't** catch me! **You're** too slow!

9

Commas

Section 1: In a list

Section 2: To avoid misunderstandings

Section 3: To separate parts of a sentence

DOI: 10.4324/9781003190455-9

SECTION 1: IN A LIST

Commas in a list

- ★ Commas separate items in a list.
- ★ Use **and** to separate the last two items on a list.

NINJABREAD GIRL'S RULES:

Commas separate items in a list to make the meaning clear.

Instead of saying:

Currants **and** cherries **and** liquorice **and** ginger.

Replace **and** with a **comma** except for the last item in the list.

Ginger**,** currants**,** cherries **and** liquorice.

KITSUNE'S WHINES:

If you don't use **commas to separate items in a list**, it can be very confusing.

Ginger currants cherries liquorice

Ninjabread Girl couldn't understand the list and got:

Ginger flavoured currants and cherry flavoured liquorice.

PUNCTUA'S POINTS:

Commas are needed to make the meaning of a **list** clear and avoid any misunderstandings.

A comma can be used instead of **and**. It signals a slight **pause** between the **words or phrases** and helps the sentence to flow and not sound too jerky.

Use **and** to separate the **last two items** on a list.

The list should have been written:

Ginger, currants, cherries and liquorice.

SECTION 2: TO AVOID MISUNDERSTANDINGS

Commas

- identify the person/ people being addressed.
- make the sentence clearer and easier to read.
- avoid any misunderstandings.

NINJABREAD GIRL'S RULES:

Commas are used to **separate the person/ people** being identified **from the rest of the sentence**.

For example:

Don't run away from me**,** Ninjabread Girl.

Don't run away from me Ninjabread Girl.

KITSUNE'S WHINES:

I thought it was funny when the Ninjutsu Trainer said,

"I like cooking my family and my pets."

I bet his family and pets were scared! He should have said,

"I like cooking**,** my family and my pets."

PUNCTUA'S POINTS:

Commas are needed to make the meaning clear and avoid any terrible misunderstandings.

The Ninjabread Girl needs to think carefully about what is being said when writing. The sentence is clearer and easier to read with a comma. It avoids misunderstandings!

Example:

"I like cooking my family and my pets." With **no comma to separate cooking from family**, this means that the Ninjutsu Trainer is talking **about cooking his family and his pets**.

"I like cooking, my family and my pets." The **comma separates cooking from family**, so the Ninjutsu Trainer **is talking about things he likes** and putting this in a list.

Example:

"Let's eat children." With **no comma to separate eat from children**, is talking **about eating children**.

"Let's eat, children." The **comma separates eat from children**, so it is **telling the children** that they should eat.

SECTION 3: TO SEPARATE PARTS OF A SENTENCE

Commas to separate parts of a sentence

Commas:

★ separate units in a sentence.
★ make the sentence clearer and easier to read.
★ avoid any misunderstandings.

NINJABREAD GIRL'S RULES

A comma is used to:

★ **separate parts of a sentence** to help make it clearer and easier to understand and avoid any misunderstandings.
★ **stop sentences from rambling** on and on without a break and making them difficult to read.
★ **add extra information** and detail.

Example:

Out of the oven, I ran.

I ran, **as fast as a cheetah**, out of the oven.

KITSUNE'S WHINES:

In the first draft, I thought it needed more detail. At least now I know how fast the Ninjabread Girl is. Now I know I can't catch her as she is as fast as a cheetah!

PUNCTUA'S POINTS:

- Too many short sentences can make your writing sound a bit jerky.
- Using a comma, you **can add extra detail** and information **to the main part of the sentence**.

For example:

I ran away. Then, I came to a river.

When I ran away, I came to a river.

When I ran away is a **subordinate clause**.

- It does not make sense on its own.
- By using a **comma**, this **subordinate clause** can be **connected to the main part of the sentence** to add more detail.

Ninjabread Girl could have written:

I leapt out of the oven. I jumped out of the window. I ran through the garden. I ran down the lane. I ran to the river.

By **using commas to link the parts of the sentences**, she could **combine** them into:

Earlier, I leapt out of the oven, jumped out of the window, ran through the garden and down the lane until I came to the river.

Tip: look out for the following **subordinate conjunctions** that help add more detail to your writing.

When, before, after, if, until

Appendix

NINJABREAD GIRL'S EDITING CHECKLIST LEVEL 1: PUNCTUATION

	I confirm when I am editing, I check that:	✓
A.	**Sentences**	
1.	My sentences make sense.	
2.	My sentences end with a full stop.	
B.	**Capital letters**	
3.	My sentences start with a capital letter.	
4.	'I' has a capital letter.	
5.	Names of people and places have a capital letter.	
6.	Names of days and months have a capital letter.	
C.	**Questions and exclamations**	
7.	I put a question mark at the end of a direct question.	
8.	I put an exclamation mark to signal a surprise or outburst.	
D.	**Speech**	
9.	I put speech marks around the words being spoken.	
10.	I started a new line when the person speaking changes.	
11.	I started the speech with a capital letter.	
	Signature: Date:	

NINJABREAD GIRL'S EDITING CHECKLIST LEVEL 2: PUNCTUATION

	I confirm when I am editing, I check that:	✓
A.	**Sentences**	
1.	My sentences are clear and easy to read.	
2.	I used a full stop, question mark or exclamation mark at the end of my sentences.	
B.	**Capital letters**	
3.	I used capital letters for "I," names of people, places, days and months.	
C.	**Apostrophes**	
4.	I used an apostrophe where something belongs to someone.	
5.	I used an apostrophe where letters are missing.	
6.	I haven't mixed up it's/its or they're/their/there.	
D.	**Commas**	
7.	I have used a comma to identify the person/people being addressed.	
8.	I have used commas to separate items in a list.	
9.	I have used commas to separate extra information from the main part of a sentence.	
	Signature: Date:	

KITSUNE'S CHALLENGE

Correct the errors:

Have you been paying attention? Do you remember the mistakes I picked out and had to correct in the Ninjabread Girl's first draft? Test your knowledge by completing my challenge. (*You can always look back to check if you are not sure.*)

1. **Correct the passage so that it makes sense**
   i jumped out of the oven i was being chased i thought i could cross the river by myself when i got closer i saw kitsune
2. **Spot the comma splicing**
   i. Read the passage aloud.
   ii. Make a mark for each unit of sense.
   iii. Insert a full stop.
      a. I looked at the river, it was moving quickly, I needed to get to the other side.
      b. Kitsune watched me, his eyes were narrow, finally he spoke.
3. **Capital letters**
   Look for 'I,' names of people, places, days and months and insert a capital letter.
   a. i jumped out of the oven and passed the ninjutsu trainer.
   b. the ninjabread girl said, "i will be back on monday."
   c. i saw kitsune long ago, he was near the river last june.
4. **Question marks – yes or no?**
   Insert either **a question mark** or **a full stop** at the end of these sentences:
   a. Where are you going
   b. Kitsune asked me if I wanted help
   c. Will you help me
   d. The Ninjutsu Trainer asked me why I ran away
   e. The Ninjabread Girl ran away quickly
   f. Could you help me over the river
5. **Exclamation marks**
   When would you use an exclamation mark?
   a. I like baking biscuits
   b. Come back here

6. Punctuate the speech

a. Hiiiiii-yaaaaa I yelled.
b. Where are you going the Ninjutsu Trainer asked.
c. You can't catch me I said loudly. I'm the Ninjabread Girl.
d. Come closer Kitsune said. By now, I could see his teeth. Will you eat me I asked. He shook his head and smiled.

7. Apostrophes

i. Insert the apostrophe in the correct place.
ii. Check its/it's and their/they're/there.
   a. Its hard to cross the river. Maybe theirs a bridge over theyre.
   b. Their is the Ninjitsu trainer. Its his voice I can hear.
   c. Theyre coming after me!

8. Commas in a list

i. Insert commas to separate the items on the list.
ii. Explore what would happen if you put the commas in the wrong place.

The Gingerbread Girl has currants for eyes cherries for her buttons and a black liquorice suit.

9. Identifying the people being addressed

Read sentences a, b and c, and discuss questions 1–3 with a partner.

a. If you run away then you will be eaten Ninjabread Girl.
b. The Ninjitsu trainer is hungry and wants to eat now Ninjabread Girl.
c. Come quickly Ninjabread Girl you need to escape.

Questions:

1. What do these sentences mean?
2. Where should the comma go?
3. How does inserting a comma change the meaning?

Certificate

EDITING LEVEL 1

awarded to

Name: ____________________

In recognition of your hard work in editing your writing.

Ninjabread Girl and Punctua ____________________

Date

Certificate

EDITING LEVEL 2

awarded to

Name: ______________________________

In recognition of your hard work in editing your writing.

Ninjabread Girl and Punctua ____________________

Date